BRITISH LIBRARY R&D REP(

Local Authority Archive Services 1992

A survey commissioned by the
Royal Commission on Historical Manuscripts
and National Council on Archives

Heather Forbes

LONDON:HMSO

ISBN 0 11 887540 X

Applications for reproduction should be made
to HMSO

Contents

Abstract

Questionnaire responses and follow-up visits form the basis of this survey, which reports on progress since a similar survey was carried out in 1985. The following areas are examined in order to give a state-of-the-art picture of local authority archive services on the eve of local government restructuring: archive services and local councils; staffing; storage; holdings and acquisitions; records management; conservation; finding aids; public access and user services; education; outreach; finance; and performance indicators. There has been a considerable growth in demand for archive services, which has been met by an increasing flexibility of response and in many cases by improved resources. However, there is a continuing unevenness of archive provision across the country and some services remain underfunded.

Acknowledgements

This project is the brainchild jointly of the National Council on Archives and the Royal Commission on Historical Manuscripts, and I am most grateful to them for the opportunity to take part. I am also indebted to the British Library Research and Development Department for financing the project, and to Hampshire County Council for allowing me four months' secondment from the Hampshire Record Office to undertake the work. This report owes much to Sonia Anderson of the Historical Manuscripts Commission who has overseen the whole project, read the drafts and made helpful suggestions for improvements. The guidance and valuable suggestions of the steering committee members (Rosemary Dunhill, Isobel Gordon, Vic Gray, Nicholas Kingsley, Christopher Kitching, Patricia Methven, Brian Smith and Arnott Wilson) are also gratefully acknowledged. Finally, I would like to thank the archivists who took part in detailed studies and all those who filled in the lengthy questionnaire, without whom this report could not have been written.

Heather Forbes
November 1992

Introduction

Over the last fifty years there has been a great expansion in the provision of publicly funded archive services in the United Kingdom in order to rescue, preserve and make available to the public a wide range of archives. These include records of local government, parishes and dioceses, landed families, businesses and societies, and some of these collections are of national or international historical importance. Record offices must be in a position to carry on with this valuable work, particularly as very high calibre material continues to come to light.

Local authority archive services are for the most part based upon permissive rather than mandatory statutory powers, which helps to explain the great diversity of archive services illustrated in this survey. In England and Wales the Local Government (Records) Act 1962 gave local authorities power to promote adequate use of records by providing public access, finding aids, talks and exhibitions, and it empowered county and county borough councils as 'principal archive authorities' to acquire other records by purchase, gift or deposit. The Local Government Act 1972 required local authorities to make proper arrangements for their own administrative records. The Public Records Act 1958, the Law of Property Act 1922 (as amended by the Law of Property (Amendment) Act 1924), the Manorial Documents Rules 1959, amended 1963 and 1967, and the Tithe Act 1936 and Tithe (Copies of Instruments of Apportionment) Rules 1960, amended 1963, stipulated rules for looking after public, manorial and tithe records and laid down a system for inspecting record offices before appointing them as suitable repositories to keep such records.

Many counties had established record offices in response to local needs before the 1962 Act; today all English and Welsh shire counties have record offices, except Avon. They usually evolved out of the central administrative department of a county council to look after its own records and those of its predecessors and are generally well established and adequately funded.

When the metropolitan counties were abolished in 1986, provision for archives was at a different level of development in each of the six metropolitan areas and Greater London, and very different outcomes have resulted. At the time there was great concern that, despite vigorous and effective campaigning, no statutory provision was made for county-wide archive services, and subsequent arrangements have thus relied upon voluntary co-operation. The Greater London Record Office has retained its London-wide role and is now administered by the City of London. Some of the metropolitan districts are working co-operatively to continue services run by the former metropolitan counties but elsewhere there are no county-wide agreements. The former metropolitan county record offices have been referred to as metropolitan counties throughout this report for brevity.

Eight shire districts have been authorised by the Secretary of State for the Environment to run archive services since 1974 when the 1972 Act came into force. Most of these services also began from a base in a central administrative department. Some remain small and under-resourced but others are well developed.

Amendments to the Local Government (Records) Act 1962 in 1963 and 1985 gave archive powers to the London boroughs and to the metropolitan boroughs respectively. Most borough and district archive services have been rooted in the local studies collections of borough libraries and museums and some already had archive collections before the amendments to the 1962 Act, particularly where the Public Libraries and Museums Act 1964, which gave some library authorities power to spend on non-book material, had been used to build up manuscript or local studies collections. By no means all the boroughs and districts have taken up archive powers and the levels of provision are very varied, although small underfunded offices predominate.

In Scotland, the Scottish Record Office played an important role in the development of archive services at the local level following the Public Records (Scotland) Act 1937 which allowed local authorities to transfer their records to the Scottish Record Office. The Local Government (Scotland) Act 1973, section 200 encouraged local authorities to make 'proper arrangements' for records belonging to them or in their custody and a government circular issued in 1974 gave guidance on section 200 stating: 'the Secretary of State expects that the new regions and islands authorities in particular will wish to maintain full scale and professionally staffed archival services for their own records'. Before this, only Dundee, Edinburgh, Glasgow and Orkney had made any provision for their records and most of the development has taken place since the implementation of the local government reorganisation in 1975. The Scottish Record Office has encouraged this development by giving professional and technical advice and by retransmitting local records to local repositories under 'charge and superintendence' agreements. Nevertheless, it could be argued that only Strathclyde offers the 'full scale' service envisaged in the 1974 local government circular. Indeed, two of the regions, Lothian and Fife, and the majority of districts, do not yet have recognisable archive services. Furthermore, the archive services provided by the nine regional and islands councils are on a much smaller scale than the established English county record office network.

In Northern Ireland, where the Public Record Office of Northern Ireland holds local as well as public and national records, there are no local authority archive services.

1992 survey: methodology

For many years the collection of comparative information has been recognised as of primary importance in the improvement of services, particularly in those areas where services have been underfunded or faced with other difficulties. This survey was designed to build on previous surveys and to supplement comparative statistics already available. It was carried out during the summer of 1992 under the auspices of the National Council on Archives and the Royal Commission on Historical Manuscripts, with funding from the British Library Research and Development Department. The aims were to identify trends since the last nation-wide survey was carried out in 1985, to provide a state-of-the-art picture of archive services on the eve of projected local government restructuring and to promote the development of performance indicators.

Questionnaires were sent to 155 local authority archive services in the United Kingdom (including branches), 114 of which (74%) submitted returns. In addition, 15 follow-up visits were carried out to supplement the responses to the questionnaires. All these services are listed in the Appendix. Separate answers were provided for record office branches in many instances, but not necessarily for every section of the questionnaire, so the total number of responding institutions will vary from section to section of this report.

The following surveys and reports have been used for purposes of comparison and to supplement findings: a survey of local archive services in England and Wales by Mr WR Serjeant for the Society of Archivists, published in the *Journal of the Society of Archivists*, 4 (October 1971), 300–26; unpublished returns of a subsequent survey by Mr Serjeant in 1980, now lodged in the Greater London Record Office; a survey of United Kingdom record repositories in 1984 carried out by the Royal Commission on Historical Manuscripts, published in the *Journal of the Society of Archivists*, 8 (April 1986), 1–16; *Standards of archive provision in London boroughs*, published by the Greater London Archives Network in 1989; final draft of a report of the London Archives Policy Working Party of 1992, entitled: 'Towards 2000 —the future of London's archives'; the annual salary returns compiled by the Society of Archivists for record repositories in the United Kingdom 1991/92; the annual statistics about county record offices in England and Wales, based on their annual estimates, compiled with the help of the Association of County Archivists and published by the Chartered Institute of Public Finance and Accountancy (CIPFA) 1991/92; the raw data for the CIPFA returns, 1992/93; and the 1990/91 statistics compiled by the Archivists of Scottish Local Authorities Working Group (ASLAWG).

Performance indicators The work of the Society of Archivists' Working Party on Performance Indicators and Standards, convened by Miss PJ Methven, has been heavily drawn upon for the performance indicators section of this report. The recommendations given in the Working Party's report to the Council of the Society of Archivists in November 1991 were used as a basis for testing performance indicators on some of the follow-up surveys. The performance indicators described in this report are all used, or being planned, by one or more of the services visited, and many, but not all of them, are based on the work of the Working Party. A revised set of recommendations relating to collection policy and development, record production and facilities, cataloguing, users and user satisfaction, and outreach was presented by the Working Party to the Society's annual conference in September 1992. Work on performance indicators for conservation and records management is now being co-ordinated by the Society's Professional Methodology Panel, which is also looking to develop more sophisticated means of measuring the quality of cataloguing.

1 Archive services and local councils

An important trend over the past decade has been the movement of many county archive services away from the central departments of the secretary or the chief executive into leisure and culture departments or directorates. WR Serjeant's survey of 1968 reported that 30 of the 35 respondent English and Welsh county archivists reported to the clerk of the county council. A similar question was not asked in 1984, but an informal survey carried out in 1985 by Patricia Bell, the then county archivist of Bedfordshire, showed that 26 of the 35 respondents remained in the chief executive's or the secretary's departments. Five of the 35 offices were independent departments, one was in the museums department and three had joined leisure departments. The present survey shows that the number of county archivists responsible to directors of leisure or of libraries and heritage is now equal to the number responsible to county secretaries, though not if these are combined with those who retain chief officer status.

Several borough and district archive services now form part of large leisure departments whilst retaining their links with libraries. In Scotland and Wales, record offices have tended to remain in the departments in which they were first established.

In the follow-up visits, opinions were sought about the advantages and disadvantages of placing a record office in a leisure or cultural department, and opinions varied. It was seen as essential for the chief archivist to retain responsibility for planning and deciding policy. Access to chief officers and councillors and to departmental meetings was also regarded as vital. Section 1.5 of the Historical Manuscripts Commission's *A standard for record repositories on constitution and finance, staff, acquisition, access*, 1990, reinforces such requirements: 'The archivist in charge should have an effective line of communication with the governing body and a position within the overall administration structure which will enable the effective promotion of the record repository's declared objectives'. The importance of retaining the distinct

Table 1

The position of archive services within their employing bodies

| | English Counties | | English Districts/Boroughs | | | | | | |
	Shire	Metro	Shire	London	Metro	Wales	Scotland	Guernsey	Total
No of returns	36	4	7	12	17	5	10	1	92
Independent department	4	1	0	0	0	1	0	1	7
Central department	15	0	5	1	0	3	4	0	28
Leisure/libraries department	15	2	2	11	15	1	6	0	52
Education department	1	0	0	0	1	0	0	0	2
Unknown/ reorganisation in progress	1	1	0	0	1	0	0	0	3

identity of the record office and the recognition of differences between archivists and fellow professionals such as librarians and museum curators were repeatedly emphasised, together with the necessity of taking a positive part in discussions about reorganisation.

A move away from the central administration could result in a lack of corporate backing for records management or council-wide information strategies. Conversely, the benefits of close liaison with museum staff, for example, are evident in Gwynedd where joint exhibition, conservation and education programmes have resulted in the attraction of additional grants, wider publicity, a higher profile and a more integrated response to the National Curriculum.

2 Staffing

Alterations in staffing levels

Over the last eight years there has been an increase of 36% in the total number of staff employed by the repositories which supplied figures for both 1984 and 1992. There has been an increase of 16% in the number of archivists and 7% in the number of conservators employed. Overall, 52 of the 92 services (branches have been included with headquarters) have more staff, 27 have the same number and eight have fewer staff than in 1984, whilst information was not available from a further five. In some cases, staff increases since 1984 have been partially reversed by later developments; four offices where staffing levels are the same as or greater than in 1984 reported staffing cuts and frozen posts, which have resulted in reduced opening hours in two cases. Difficulties in recruiting qualified archivists have been experienced in a few offices (e.g. Nottinghamshire, Isle of Wight) and it is not always easy to fill the other half of job-share schemes (e.g. Hammersmith & Fulham, Lambeth). The increases in staffing were not evenly spread. The shire counties have put proportionally the most resources into increased staffing and the metropolitan counties and the shire districts the least.

Since 1984, reader numbers have risen by a mean average of 59%. This has had a direct impact on services, because record office users are more 'labour intensive' than museum visitors or even library users as they require a greater degree of attention in the form of expert advice, supervision and the production of records from the strongroom. Several offices (e.g. Derbyshire, Dorset, Lancashire, West Sussex) quoted the increase in visitor numbers, or the need for increased security in the search room, as the reason for staff increases. Many of the increases resulted from offices taking on new functions or offering a wider range of services such as archive education (e.g. Wolverhampton), records management (e.g. Chester, Cumbria, Shropshire, Staffordshire), or film and sound archives (e.g. Hampshire, Lancashire). Staff had also been appointed to help with cataloguing backlogs (e.g. Dorset, Hampshire, Oxfordshire, Suffolk), computerisation (e.g. London Guildhall, Gwynedd) or conservation and preservation (e.g. Birmingham, Cheshire, Edinburgh, Lancashire). Not all the new posts were funded by councils, as was shown by the appointment of self-financing researchers (e.g. in Essex, Gloucestershire, Lincolnshire, West Sussex) or self-financing archivists for particular tasks (e.g. Edinburgh) and by grant-aided cataloguing and conservation projects (e.g. Birmingham, Lincolnshire, Tyne & Wear, Warwickshire).

The number of staff employed in the various categories of repository varies tremendously and the median numbers of the full staffing establishment and of archivists and conservators are as follows: counties, a total of 16.4 staff, including six archivists and two conservators; metropolitan counties (the West Yorkshire branches have been included with the headquarters return), a total of 14.9 staff, including 4.4 archivists and 2.5 conservators; shire districts a total of five staff including two archivists and no conservator; London boroughs, a total of 2.75 staff including one archivist and no conservator; metropolitan districts, a total of 3.5 staff including one archivist and no conservator; Wales, a total of 10 staff including four archivists and one conservator; Scotland, a total of two staff including one archivist and no conservator. Five of the repositories responding to the questionnaire (two London boroughs, one metropolitan district, and two in Scotland) had no professional archivists. The report *Standards of archive provision in London boroughs* showed that 16 London repositories (53%) had no professionally qualified archivists on their staff in 1989. Archivists have since been appointed in at least two boroughs—Sutton and Croydon—but the lack of professional staff, and understaffing in general, remains a major problem in many London boroughs. This extract from the 1992 report *Towards 2000—the future of London's archives* describes some of the problems, which also exist in understaffed offices in other parts of the country: 'In instances of one-person operated services search rooms can be subject to unforeseen closures due to staff leave or sickness and appointment systems are essential. Services have in some instances been severely disrupted to the point of the public having no access to the archives at all. On the other hand in cases where long opening hours are maintained the public may suffer from the lack of availability of a professional archivist for much of the time, or of adequate lists and indexes.'

Table 2
Staff employed in record repositories in 1991/92*

| | English Counties | | English Districts/Boroughs | | | | | | |
	Shire	Metro	Shire	London	Metro	Wales	Scotland	Guernsey	Total
No of returns	38	4	7	12	17	6	10	1	95
Archivists	245	26.6	17	26.5	24	25.5	15	1	380.6
Conservators	69.4	10	3	7	8	5	2	0	104.4
Records managers	25.2	0.2	1	1	1	3	1	1	33.4
Education officers	10.3	1	0	1	3	1	1	0	17.3
Technical	47.1	1.7	0	7	7.1	3	2	0	67.9
Total staff	654.2	61.4	44	58.8	69.8	64.7	37.5	4	994.4

Note: CIPFA returns were used to fill gaps for Durham, Dyfed and Humberside.

* Respondents were not asked to distinguish between the number of employees and the tasks upon which they were engaged. Some archivists who are also records managers appear only as archivists. In addition, education officers who work for archive services but are paid by other departments are not generally included.

Performance indicators and standards

Sections 2.1 to 2.5 of *A standard for record repositories* provide guidelines on minimum staffing levels.

Staff input is a vital component of many performance indicators. It was considered relatively easy to measure where staff carried out the same task all or most of the time, but could be difficult where individuals undertook a range of activities or where staff were shared with another section. Time sheets seemed to be widely disliked but time diaries for specific tasks or periodic spot checks were used by some of the archivists visited to calculate, for instance, the proportions of time spent on cataloguing, records management and running the public service.

3 Storage

Capacity

As was pointed out in the 1984 report, 'the storage capacity of repositories apparently similar in character is markedly varied'. In 1992, capacities range from $0.5m^3$ to $2,250m^3$, with a median average of $368.5m^3$. It is not possible to provide figures for total capacity of the responding repositories due to the recent but still incomplete transition to measurements in cubic metres, not yet adopted by 30 repositories. Archives comprise 81% of total holdings, modern records 18%, and other, unspecified holdings 1%. Across the repositories as a whole, a median of $10m^3$ is vacant. Details of accessions in 1991/92 measured in cubic metres ranging from 0 to $94m^3$ were provided by 68 services. The mean average is $18m^3$ and the median $11m^3$. Accessions are notoriously unpredictable and fluctuate widely from year to year but accession rates over a number of years can be used as a rough and ready aid to forward planning.

Of the 102 repositories which supplied figures, 24% are already full, 52% estimate that they will be full in 5 years and 11% that they will be full in 10 years. Despite the fact that there have been over 40 new record office buildings or extensions since 1984, only 13% of local authority repositories do not envisage a storage problem over the next decade. This is only 1% less than in 1984.

Table 3
Storage

In each case the first figure is the number of repositories concerned, the figure in brackets the number with a firm commitment for additional storage:

| | English Counties | | English Districts/Boroughs | | | | | | |
	Shire	Metro	Shire	London	Metro	Wales	Scotland	Guernsey	Total
No of returns	40	9	7	12	17	6	10	1	102
Full now	9(7)	3	2	2(1)	4	3	2(1)	0	25(9)
Full in 5 years	15(4)	6	4	9(2)	9(2)	3	7(3)	0	53(11)
Full in 10 years	7(2)	0	0	1	2	0	0	1	11(2)

Out-stores

Out-stores are in many cases far from an ideal solution as they frequently offer lower standards of storage, pose security problems and reduce accessibility of the records stored there. However, 37 repositories use out-stores: 23 for archive holdings; five for records management; and nine for both. The amounts stored range from 2% to 73% of total holdings, with a mean average of 27%. The situation has improved since 1984 as only 36% of services have out-stores (69% in 1984). Similarly, only three services (11 in 1984) have over 60% of their holdings in out-stores in 1992, and 65 services have no material out-housed.

Sub-standard storage

To quote from section 7.1 of BS 5454, *Recommendations for storage and exhibition of archival documents*: 'Unsuitable environments have damaged documents more extensively than any other single factor' and yet the problem of sub-standard storage continues. Thirty-one respondents reported that their main storage did not broadly conform to the standards recommended in BS 5454. Forty-four noted that their out-stores did not conform. Only 11 offices could report firm commitments to bring the storage up to standard. The lack of proper environmental controls was the most widespread problem reported, particularly in the London and metropolitan boroughs and in Scotland. In the shire counties problems occurred most commonly in out-stores. No capital grants are available to improve record storage and the money has not been provided by the councils concerned to remedy the situation.

Taking the country as a whole, a mean average of 43% of archival storage (including out-stores) is provided with air conditioning, 89% with fire detection and alarm equipment, 18% with automatic fire extinguishing equipment and 73% with intruder alarms. Forty-one offices have no air conditioning equipment and a number of them reported fluctuating temperature and humidity readings. Some of the more recently built new record offices, such as Suffolk, have been designed to achieve stable environmental conditions through high thermal inertia. All offices, except for one Welsh and three London repositories, have fire detection devices but only 26 have automatic fire extinguishing equipment. More disturbing is the fact that 17 do not have intruder alarms.

Specialist storage

Seventy-one respondents (73%) held films, videos, or records in audio or electronic format, usually only in small quantities, but only 12 (12%) had specialist storage available. Furthermore, only 19 repositories offer

Table 4

Sub-standard storage

| | English Counties | | English Districts/Boroughs | | | | | | |
	Shire	Metro	Shire	London	Metro	Wales	Scotland	Guernsey	Total
No of returns	38	9	7	12	17	5	10	1	99
Main storage sub-standard	4	5	2	7	7	1	5	0	31
Out-storage sub-standard	18	7	1	6	7	2	2	1	44
Commitment to improvements	4	0	0	2	4	0	1	0	11

Table 5
Specialist storage

	English Counties		English Districts/Boroughs			Wales	Scotland	Guernsey	Total
	Shire	Metro	Shire	London	Metro				
No of returns	36	9	7	12	17	5	10	1	97
Storage of:									
film/video	22	7	6	11	12	4	3	1	66
audio	22	5	4	10	11	3	4	0	59
electronic	9	0	1	3	0	2	0	0	15
Specialist storage	9	1	1	0	1	0	0	0	12
Consultation facilities for:									
audio-visual	6	3	1	3	4	0	2	0	19
electronic	0	0	0	0	0	0	0	0	0

facilities for consultation of audio-visual records and none provide facilities for looking at records in an electronic format. Section 3.9 of the Historical Manuscripts Commission's *A standard for record repositories* states: 'Records in a format or medium requiring special equipment for their consultation (such as microfilm, microfiche, audio-visual and machine-readable records) should not be acquired unless the record repository has, or plans soon to obtain, the necessary equipment, or is able to arrange facilities for appropriate public access elsewhere under proper invigilation.' Further provision is clearly required for the storage and consultation of such records, perhaps on a regional basis as suggested by one of the archivists visited.

4 Holdings and acquisitions

Respondents were asked to calculate approximate percentages of their holdings that were (1) administrative records of the parent authority, including predecessors, (2) other local authority records, (3) designated public records (including 'charge and superintendence' records in Scotland), (4) gifts and purchases, and (5) loans and deposits (including ecclesiastical records). Taking into account the total bulk of holdings reported by respondents, administrative records comprised 23%, other local authority records 15%, public records 11%, gifts and purchases 7% and deposits 44%. There were regional variations such as a higher proportion of administrative records in the shire districts and in Scotland and greater percentages of loans and deposits in the shire, metropolitan and Welsh counties. Although the overall proportion of purchases and deposits is considerably greater than that of gifts, 53 repositories reported that they encouraged gifts in preference to deposits.

Fifty-six repositories had written acquisitions policies and a further 11 were planning to introduce them. The policies generally cover the statutory basis for acquisition, the conditions of receipt and a definition of the types of record and the geographical area considered appropriate for collection. Some lay down target categories such as business records or list areas where other repositories are collecting, with a view to avoiding competition. Nevertheless, competition was reported by 26 repositories. Where further details were given, universities and museums featured most, although demarcation disputes were reported in two metropolitan areas and by two shire district record offices. The recommendation in section 3.4 of *A standard for record repositories* to deposit written acquisitions policies with the Royal Commission on Historical Manuscripts and to make them publicly available in the record offices may help to clarify the situation. The *Code of practice on archives in museums* agreed by the Museums Association, the Society of Archivists and the Association of Independent Museums has already helped to ease problems in this area.

All but eight repositories maintain an accessions register in accordance with section 3.12 of *A standard for record repositories*. Twelve have computerised their accessions registers and a further 11 plan to do so. Formal deposit agreements are used by 54 repositories and planned by nine more.

Gifts and deposits are actively solicited by 64 repositories. The obligation in England under the Parochial Registers and Records Measure (1978, amended 1992) to carry out inspections every five (formerly six) years has helped to ensure a good coverage of Church of England records in repositories approved as diocesan record offices. Systematic surveys of records for which there is no statutory basis for deposit were also reported in the following areas: nonconformist, school, business, community council, parish council, charity, military and family records. Newspapers are monitored particularly for business closures, and letters, sometimes with a publicity leaflet, are sent to target groups such as solicitors, businesses and politicians. The maintenance of a high profile generally and the importance of outreach activities were emphasised by several archivists. Talks, press releases, radio interviews, displays and publicity leaflet campaigns all have their part to play. Eleven offices commented that lack of storage space or staff dictated a reactive rather than a pro-active collecting policy. This is unfortunate because material needs to be collected to fill gaps in collections retrospectively and to ensure that current activities are adequately recorded for the historians of the future.

Seventeen offices reported that 'substantial or significant loans/deposits' had been reclaimed for sale by their owners since 1985. Some of these collections had subsequently been bought by the repositories concerned, with the help of the Government Purchase Grant Funds or the National Heritage Memorial Fund. These funds enabled over 20 local authority archive services to purchase important local records in the year 1991/92, and only six repositories reported failure to purchase major collections due to a lack of funds since 1985. Five noted that the funding shortfall was local and only one that national funding had not been forthcoming.

Performance indicators

The basic standards such as the existence of a written acquisitions policy are already met by over 50% of repositories. In contrast, very few of the offices visited currently calculate time spent on soliciting or even processing accessions.

5 Records management

Forty-eight of the 97 respondents are responsible for records management within their authorities, and in Tyne & Wear, where the county council has been abolished, a comprehensive records management system is offered to all the districts. The breakdown of repositories operating records management is as follows: 25 shire counties, three metropolitan counties, four shire districts, three London boroughs, six metropolitan districts, four Welsh counties, three Scottish councils and Guernsey. Nineteen of the repositories offering records management now belong to leisure or library departments although at least eight of these repositories had developed the service whilst in central departments. Twenty-five offices run their records management operations from separate records centres.

A full service with transfer of records from departments to the records centre, retention schedules and retrieval, appraisal and review, confidential destruction and transfer of records to archives is offered by 32 repositories. Fully-fledged records management systems ensure the preservation of an adequate record of the work of the authority. They also provide efficient, cost-effective systems for dealing with semi-current and non-current records which might otherwise be abandoned in a basement, destroyed prematurely or microfilmed indiscriminately if office space became tight. In Tyne & Wear, the existence of the records management operation helped when the records of the old metropolitan county council came to be divided up, as departments did not have to sort through piles of unnecessary paperwork or dispute the ownership of files.

Nine offices operate a registry or current filing system for all or part of the parent authority. This has the advantage of providing efficient control of records from their creation to destruction but can result in archival staff being called in to cover for registry staff.

Seventeen offices offer record storage only. Several repositories are in the process of surveying departmental records or carrying out feasibility studies for the implementation of full records management services (e.g. Warwickshire, Isle of Wight). Supplementary comments disclosed that a lack of corporate backing, staff, or storage space prevented at least 11 repositories from offering records management. User groups have been established by five repositories.

Only five repositories reported that another department ran the records management service and these operations were generally limited to storage facilities only. In Croydon records management and the archives service were seen as separate activities, and the storage and retrieval of semi-current records were contracted out to a commercial firm at about the time the first archivist was appointed. Inter-departmental approaches can be helpful. In Chester the records manager goes on joint visits to departments with the person employed by the Management Services Advisory Unit to study work methods. An information strategy spearheaded jointly by the record office and the information technology department is also planned.

Recharging

The recharging of departments using the records management system has been introduced by 10 repositories. Recharges are usually formulated in proportion to the space taken up by each department's

8

records, but sometimes take into consideration the number of documents retrieved. Income from recharges is seen as a means of funding the records manager's post in future in one London borough, where the leisure and recreation department has withdrawn financing for the salary. Tyne & Wear is the only office to have introduced service level agreements, although at least eight offices are planning to do so.

Work for other bodies

Twenty-five repositories store records or carry out records management work for other local authorities. Several shire counties provide a service to the districts and some of the former metropolitan counties do work for the districts, ex-authorities or the new joint boards. In Scotland, Dundee acts on an agency basis for Tayside region. Eleven offices offer services to private bodies, ranging from Citizens' Advice Bureaux to businesses. The service to private bodies is particularly well developed in Tyne & Wear. After the abolition of the metropolitan county council, more space became available in the records centre. In order to make best use of the resources available, and to generate income, private firms were invited to use the service. Charges are levied by 10 repositories for services offered to private bodies and other local authorities but details of charges are usually confidential for commercial reasons.

Private storage firms

Private storage firms are not generally considered an attractive alternative by the offices visited as the firms offer a very different service with high charges for withdrawals and no advice on disposal. Fears were expressed, however, by those repositories paying very high charges for their accommodation.

Performance indicators

Quantitative measures used by records managers visited include calculations of the number of boxes received, processed, reviewed and destroyed per user department for a specified period. A comparison of the number of boxes transferred with the number destroyed showed overall increases or decreases in holdings and can be used to identify potential storage problems. Statistics are also kept for the number of documents issued to individual user departments.

Qualitative measures are more difficult to apply but can include the percentage of holdings transferred to archives and annual turnover rates in the records centre. Calculations of annual turnover rates should take into account the proportion of records too recent to destroy and records such as adoption files with very long closure periods. One of the performance targets of the chief archivist in Tyne & Wear is to ensure that there is no more than 1% vacant space in the records centre. This figure is designed to ensure that maximum use is made of the space available by matching inflow of records with outflow whilst allowing room for a fairly large emergency deposit.

6 Conservation

In-house facilities

There were 97 respondents to this question and 60 have in-house conservation facilities (62%). There are no in-house conservation facilities in two shire counties, one metropolitan county, five shire districts, five London boroughs, eleven metropolitan districts, two Welsh counties, and all but one of the Scottish regions and districts. Many of these, however, share facilities elsewhere (see below), and where branch record offices exist, it is more usual to share the conservation facilities at the headquarters than to provide separate facilities at each branch.

Three repositories (two London boroughs and a Welsh county) appear to have made no provision for conservation at all, noting no recourse to commercial facilities or to sharing the facilities of another repository. A further six repositories (one metropolitan county, three metropolitan districts, a Scottish region and a Scottish district) reported that no conservation work was done during the course of the year and financial pressures were cited as the reason, if any comment was made.

Shared facilities

Joint schemes mainly operate in metropolitan areas and where city record offices have no conservator. In Chester, where the city record office contributes financially to the county record office's conservation unit, a legal contract was drawn up covering all areas of work to be undertaken with performance measures, payment agreements and arrangements for arbitration. The main benefits the city derives from sharing facilities rather than using a commercial firm are access to staff training and day-to-day advice and the undertaking of a conservation survey. Disaster planning is another area which is being developed. The implementation and monitoring of performance measures and detailed time sheets are vital for the success of the scheme. A value for money evaluation has also been carried out.

Joint schemes also operate in South Yorkshire, where Sheffield carries out conservation work for Barnsley, Doncaster and Rotherham, and in Greater Manchester where the county record office has an arrangement with some of the district services in the area.

Such co-operative ventures could perhaps be used to much greater effect in Greater London and some of the other metropolitan areas, particularly where existing facilities are not used to their full capacity. If a fully integrated system is not practical, the co-ordination of planning for emergencies or the bulk purchase of materials could perhaps be investigated.

Successful integration of resources with the library and museums services was also reported in Berkshire and Gwynedd respectively. In Gwynedd, the arrangement has made possible successful grant applications to the Area Museum Council for photographic conservation.

Commercial facilities

Commercial facilities are used by 26 of the record offices without in-house facilities but are also used by 10 record offices to supplement their own facilities. Bookbinding is the work most often farmed out but in a few of these offices, most notably the Guildhall Library in London, funding is available for the use of commercial facilities to supplement the amount of work that can be completed during the year by the in-house conservators.

In the absence of in-house facilities in many Scottish repositories, commercial firms are widely used. Strathclyde is the only local authority record office with full-time conservators and it does not have the spare capacity to undertake work for other authorities on a regular basis. Occasional jobs, particularly on 'charge and superintendence' records are sent by offices without conservators to the Scottish Record Office but again there is insufficient spare capacity to deal with all local authority records. A large proportion of the work in Scotland is therefore done by commercial firms in Falkirk and Larbert, or by a conservator at Dundee University. Sometimes long delays have been experienced due to the quantities of work undertaken.

Number of conservators and workbenches

The number of conservators employed has no correlation with the total holding of records or with the percentage of records too fragile for production. Where calculations of the conservation backlog have been made, it has been estimated, for example, that 100 man years would be needed to rectify the problem in one repository alone.

A comparison of the number of conservators with the number of workbenches shows that just under half the repositories have no room for further conservation staff and this obviously restricts any expansion of staff levels. However, if all the conservation units are taken together, only 74% of workbenches are occupied. The comparative figure for 1984 is 68%. Allowing for the fact that other staff are being brought into the work of the conservation section to a greater extent than formerly, the number of 'free' places drops slightly but there is still room to employ or train more conservators to help reduce the enormous workload.

Conservation budgets and grants

It was noticeable that it was in services without their own conservators that cuts to the conservation budget were most frequently reported. One London borough commented that the conservation figures were 'not representative as nearly all work was caught up in the expenditure freeze'. A shire district wrote: 'We have no budget for conservation work. The very limited amount we can afford to have done . . . is funded entirely from donations'. Similar problems are forecast in one shire county office where financial cutbacks seem likely to obliterate the conservation budget in 1993/94. As a result great emphasis is being placed on preservation.

In some of the smaller services with the most constrained budgets a real tension was recorded between spending on conservation and spending to alleviate unsatisfactory storage conditions. One archivist also commented that conservation grants would only be given when the grantors were satisfied with storage conditions.

Since the last survey two new trust funds awarding conservation grants have been established. The National Manuscripts Conservation Trust, founded in 1990, has already awarded grants to 11 local authorities, including £37,800 over three years to the Yorkshire Archaeological Society (part of the West Yorkshire Archives Service) towards the conservation of the court rolls of the manor of Wakefield. In addition, seven repositories reported that they had made successful applications to the Wolfson Foundation, which set up a document preservation and purchase fund in 1986. Sixteen repositories have gained grants from other sources, including the Scottish Record Office Conservation Grant. This latter has, however, remained at the same level for some years, effectively eroding the benefit of what can be achieved with it. Two

Scottish archivists also expressed concern about the fact that the National Manuscripts Conservation Trust and the Scottish Record Office Conservation Grant are almost exclusively for deposits and gifts rather than records of the authority itself, which may cause further problems in Scotland where higher proportions of administrative records are held.

Conservation surveys and documents unfit to be produced

Very few offices could provide an accurate figure for the proportion of documents unfit to be produced to the public and the comments revealed some of the difficulties, such as the impossibility of quantifying the problem without opening every box and package, and the varying interpretations of 'unfit'. Thirty-eight respondents could not supply a figure at all and most others estimated that unfit material amounted to less than 5% of their holdings, as was the case in the 1985 survey. More offices recorded the number of items unfit for production by way of repair forms compiled by archivists when accessioning or cataloguing.

Conservation surveys should help to identify and quantify the arrears of all categories of conservation requirements, not just those documents which are too fragile to be produced. Surveys have been carried out, or are in process of being carried out, in 35% of services (nineteen shire counties, four shire districts, four London boroughs and four metropolitan districts, Highland region, Nithsdale district, and Guernsey). No conservation surveys were noted in the metropolitan counties or Wales. The scope and nature of the surveys varies from limited surveys with a specific purpose, such as the survey of parish registers in the Isle of Wight which formed the basis of a successful bid for grant aid for their repair, to an all encompassing survey being carried out at Cheshire which will take many years to complete. This survey, which has brought to light a massive repair backlog, is already making a more systematic flow of repair work possible and is also providing the opportunity to rectify packaging problems.

Preservation

The replies concerning preservation demonstrate that correct storage, boxing, packaging and handling of archives have been given a much higher profile over the past ten years. Six years was the average (median) given for the implementation of such measures. Surrey reported that 'additional staff were acquired in 1989 to bring preventative conservation to a high standard. Before that, packaging standards had been considerably improved over a period of years but were subject to staffing constraints'. Derbyshire commented that such work was 'an integral part of the work of the conservation section. Conservation assistant employed almost exclusively on cleaning and wrapping . . . Preventative conservation also included in outreach events, e.g. open days'. The interviews carried out also revealed an increasing involvement of conservators, and indeed of all other repository staff, with all aspects of preservation. Disaster plans and training (where quick action could save thousands of pounds in conservation costs), general staff training about handling and packaging, and the monitoring of conditions in strongrooms are carried out by most conservators, and microfilming and photographic work are also dealt with by some conservators. Ensuring the correct environmental conditions is an important prerequisite to traditional conservation work and proper packaging probably has more effect on ensuring that the bulk of records survive than any conservation work carried out without reference to a wider preservation policy.

Reprographics

Reprographics are increasingly seen as an integral part of a conservation programme, both as a preventative measure and as an alternative to conservation in certain circumstances. Seventy-two of the 97 respondents (74%) provide copies of their most frequently used records for consultation by the public, thus saving wear and tear on the originals. Five have no microform readers and the remaining 20 have some records available in microform but not necessarily their most heavily used records. The use of transcripts, photographs and photocopies was also noted by several offices. In Scotland less recourse has been had to microform copies because the most heavily used genealogical resources, such as testamentary records and parish registers, are kept centrally at the Office of the Registrar General and the Scottish Record Office, and other genealogical resources, such as copies of the census, are more usually kept in local studies libraries.

Parish registers are the most common records to be available in microform. The work of the Church of Jesus Christ of Latter-Day Saints (Mormons) in providing additional copies for public consultation must be recognised here. Microform copies of nonconformist, probate and land tax records are frequently available and other popular classes of records to be provided in microform include electoral registers, newspapers, tithe and enclosure awards, rate books, Ordnance Survey maps and selected quarter sessions records.

Of the services which noted the form in which copies of their most heavily used documents were supplied, 49% provided predominantly microfilm, 23% mainly microfiche, 21% offered both and 7% transcripts, photographs or photocopies. The predominance of microfilm may be due partly to early investment in microfilm readers and partly to this being the format favoured by the Mormons. Essex noted that films produced by the Mormons were being converted into fiche format and a number of other services have followed this route.

Since 1984, when only 12 respondents reported sending copies to libraries, the dissemination of microform copies has become more widespread. Thirty-three repositories make copies available in libraries or museums, or are planning to do so, 16 in other record offices, and 26 sell copies to individuals. Only four offices (six in 1984) loan copies to individuals but again usually only in exceptional circumstances.

The interpretation of whether or not microform and photographic facilities were provided in-house varied as some respondents interpreted in-house to mean within the employing organisation whereas others did not. However, the general picture which emerged was that 42% of the repositories answering this question had in-house microform facilities and 41% had in-house photographic facilities. The use of commercial firms to supplement in-house facilities was quite common, particularly for colour photography and the development of black and white photographs. A few offices reported running a microfilm unit for their employing body (e.g. Berkshire, Gwynedd and Suffolk), the former two in connection with the records management services run for the councils concerned. Only 11 repositories used no micrographic services (five of them had no microform readers) and only five repositories did not use photographic services.

Performance indicators

The question concerning the number of items repaired in 1991/92 attracted the most criticism and demonstrated that statistics used in conservation work are not readily comparable. Essex, which recorded the highest number of jobs, noted that individual pieces of paper were counted as items whereas Doncaster, which had one of the lowest figures, reported that two boxes of single-sheet sixteenth and seventeenth-century papers counted as one item. Record office annual reports show that the work of the conservation section tends to be reported in terms of numbers of books bound, maps encapsulated, documents cleaned and so on, rather than the number of uniform units processed and even comparisons from year to year within one office are not easy as the time spent conserving two different volumes can vary enormously. A more sophisticated measure than number of jobs is clearly required, together with some nationally agreed basic standards upon which an assessment of quality can be based. Work on these areas is currently being co-ordinated by the Professional Methodology Panel of the Society of Archivists.

Some work towards suitable performance measures has been carried out in three of the offices visited. In Cheshire detailed time sheets are filled in and in Berkshire a system of measuring work in units of time is being developed. Conservation standards are also being drafted in Berkshire as part of a quality audit. In Warwickshire estimates of time and materials are included on all job sheets and on the survey sheets for all new accessions partly in order to allocate priorities but also to analyse the cost-effectiveness of the treatments. Such calculations are vital when the service is under threat but can also be used to present a bid for additional resources. The recording of the conservation work required on all new accessions also provides additional useful measures such as the amount of work generated by one year of accessions compared with the amount of work completed, the cost of a year's acquisitions in conservation terms and so on. Over time it should be possible to calculate the average time it takes to repair particular types of document damage and to compare estimates of time and cost with the actual time taken.

7 Finding aids

The backlog problem

Forty-one repositories have carried out a survey of uncatalogued holdings and a further five plan to do so. Such surveys quantify the nature of the problem and allow systematic and prioritised cataloguing of the backlog. Large cataloguing and indexing backlogs were reported by most offices from all categories of local authority archive services. With the national average of only 53% of holdings fully catalogued, 23% uncatalogued and only 46% indexed by personal name, 58% by place name and 50% by subject, there is clearly an enormous problem which needs addressing. Indexing backlogs exist in all but 10 offices. A few offices deliberately do not maintain personal name indexes and other offices are struggling to build up all indexes where they have not been previously kept. In five offices (Croydon, Greenwich, Kirklees, Wakefield and Wolverhampton) over 50% of the holdings are uncatalogued. The problem is getting worse in 52% of those offices providing measurements in cubic metres as the quantity of new accessions exceeded the quantity of records catalogued during the year. Sixteen cubic metres were catalogued in 1991/92 on average across the country but eighteen were received. One Welsh county, one London borough and one metropolitan district reported that no records had been catalogued during 1991/92. The presence across the UK of such a large and growing proportion of unlisted records has serious implications for searchers, who are generally denied access to uncatalogued records, and for depositors, who probably received only the briefest summary of the records when they were deposited. There is undoubtedly a growing awareness of the problem and perception of its unacceptability and several offices have worked consistently over a number of years towards a solution.

Tackling the problem   A wide range of methods is being employed to tackle the problem. The most obvious solution is to appoint new staff, either archivists to do the cataloguing, or archive assistants for search room and other duties to free archivists for cataloguing. At least six respondents have appointed new, permanent staff to help reduce cataloguing backlogs. In addition, 11 services have appointed archivists on a fixed term for this purpose and 17 have applied successfully for grant aid to reduce cataloguing arrears. Only certain categories of records attract funding, and these might not be the archivist's highest priority so this solution needs to be part of a wider approach. In Tyne & Wear, for example, medical records subject to an extended closure period are being catalogued with outside funding because they are vital to a study on infant health.

Some of the offices visited use archive assistants or trainee archivists for the more straightforward listing, particularly where guidelines have been drawn up, and 55 repositories use voluntary labour. Many volunteers, however, concentrate on producing valuable finding aids for genealogists, such as indexes to parish registers, rather than producing basic catalogues.

The regrettable tendency for cataloguing to take second place to more immediately pressing demands, such as increased public use of the search room, has led to the re-examination of procedures in some offices. As a result, some archivists have been appointed or redeployed purely to catalogue. In Hampshire, archivists are regularly given 'free for cataloguing' periods of two weeks to devote to cataloguing with as few interruptions as possible. In Essex, archivists at Chelmsford spend six months each year in the 'Public Services Team' and then six months in the 'Acquisitions Team' where more time is made available for cataloguing. Cataloguing targets and basic time diaries are used to monitor progress and gradual increases in time devoted to cataloguing are proving possible. The more radical solution of closing the search room for one day a week in order to free staff for cataloguing has been chosen by a few offices. A number of offices have a policy to accession and catalogue in full as large a percentage as possible of the records as soon as they arrive. This is achieved in Gwynedd by having an archivist dedicated to this task, and in Hampshire by having a rota of archivists to deal with, and list, all accessions for two-week blocks. The careful selection and weeding of archives before they reach the record office was emphasised in Tyne & Wear. Cataloguing manuals have been compiled by a number of offices (e.g. Gwynedd) and box listing is seen by at least 35 offices as part of the solution for certain collections.

Computers offer the opportunity for more efficient cataloguing and indexing but have not been adopted widely mainly because of the financial investment necessary and the lack of software able to cope with the different cataloguing levels. A number of offices have recently developed or commissioned their own software. Some programmes have been marketed more widely, such as MODES (Archives) which has been developed by archivists at the British Antarctic Survey, and ARCHWAY which has been recently developed for Portsmouth City Records Office and is based on the cataloguing conventions laid down in the *Manual of archival description, second edition,* by Michael Cook and Margaret Procter. Computers are used by 15 offices for cataloguing and indexing, by five offices for indexing only and by 29 offices for cataloguing only whilst 10 further offices are planning to computerise lists or indexes or both. The returns on computerised cataloguing are misleading as it is clear from some comments given on the questionnaire, and from Robert Chell's *Directory of computer applications in archives,* 1992, that many of these offices are using word-processing facilities only.

Indexing backlogs are being addressed in some offices by farming out more straightforward indexes to archive assistants or volunteers. In Bedfordshire, Gloucestershire and Staffordshire the problem has never arisen because material is always indexed after cataloguing. On-line or computer-generated hard copy indexes automatically produced from computerised catalogues clearly remove the problem of indexing backlogs for the future.

Published guides

Forty-one offices have published guides to their holdings but many are long out of date. One archivist noted that the use of a computer with a desk-top publishing package would ease the problem of keeping such guides up to date in the light of the constant flow of new material that all record offices experience.

Performance indicators

Performance indicators covering finding aids have already been introduced in some of the offices visited and include measurements of cataloguing output by cataloguing units (usually analogous to production units) and by bulk, number of catalogues indexed, and time spent cataloguing each year. Bedfordshire has a detailed form addressing degree of difficulty, the level at which the records have been catalogued, time taken, number of index entries and so on. Measuring cataloguing output in cubic metres is not thought practical by some offices, particularly those which mainly attract small accessions, shelve accessions randomly or use a large variety of different sized boxes. However, 55 repositories were able to provide cataloguing figures in cubic metres and this method does have the advantage of facilitating comparison of bulk catalogued with bulk of new accessions and so indicating whether the backlog is increasing. Qualitative measurements of cataloguing have proved difficult to implement and further work is currently being undertaken by the Professional Methodology Panel of the Society of Archivists.

Other benefits of performance indicators include the ability to make year on year comparisons of cataloguing and indexing output, to compare with other repositories and to analyse whether methods to increase output are working. Total staff time spent cataloguing can be valuable for checking that cataloguing is being given sufficient priority in the work schedule, for calculating costs of cataloguing, and for producing informed estimates of how long particular types of records might be expected to take to catalogue, which could in turn be useful for planning work schedules and targets.

8 Public access and user services

Growth in use

In 1991/92 the total number of reader visits to the 96 repositories providing visitor statistics was 478,723. The mean average visitor figures were as follows: shire counties, 7,268; metropolitan counties, 3,488; shire districts, 2,818; London boroughs, 3,196; metropolitan boroughs, 4,927; Wales, 3,300; and Scotland, 1,597. In record offices which supplied figures for 1979, 1984 and 1992, there has been a total increase of 99% since 1979 and 38% since 1984. Some repositories have seen considerably greater increases than this and the mean average increase since 1984 was 59%. Repositories experienced an even greater growth in the number of postal enquiries concerning archives, with a total increase of 127% since 1979 and of 58% since 1984. They also received a mean average of 2,476 telephone enquiries about documentary holdings, and produced a mean average of 13,089 documents and 12,682 microforms during 1991/92. Comparisons with 1979 and 1984 are not possible for telephone enquiries or productions as the relevant questions were not asked previously, but annual reports point to steady increases over the period in question.

Facilities

The number of reader spaces available ranges from 4 to 120, with a mean average of 26. On average, a third of the total seats are given over to microform, although in North Yorkshire where most holdings are available for inspection only on microform 88% of the spaces available are for microform. Reader spaces and microform facilities in Scotland are generally much lower. Booking is necessary or advised in 38 offices, and at least 6 more offices recommend booking microform machines. In some offices (e.g. Essex) where seat occupancy rates are very high, it is necessary to book several days in advance in order to ensure a seat. In a few of the smallest offices (e.g. Merseyside), one does not necessarily have to book a seat but it is advisable to make an appointment to ensure that a member of staff is available.

Opening hours range from 11.25 to 61 per week, with a mean average of 37. The longest and shortest opening hours tend to be in library-based services. London and metropolitan borough archive services comprise 19 out of the 28 offices which open on Saturdays and at least one evening a week. Twenty-four offices open at least one evening a week but not on Saturdays and 21 open on a Saturday but not in the evening. Forty-seven offices produce documents on demand throughout the day, except for the last 15 or 30 minutes in some cases. Twenty-five offices do not produce documents over the lunch period and a further 12 require advance orders for evening or Saturday openings. More irregular breaks in production are caused by staff shortages, documents being required from outstores, the presence of only one member of staff on duty, and, in Lewisham, the presence of a school group, for example, which would prevent documents from being produced for other searchers. Three offices reported the use of fixed production times, 30 or 45 minutes apart.

Seventy-eight repositories are accessible to wheelchair users but 23 are not. County Archive Research Network (CARN) cards are used in 29 offices, other tickets are used in 16 offices and all but four offices uphold the principle of free access. Thirty-five offices offer special facilities for consulting maps and 19 for audio-visual materials and (as already stated) none for electronic media.

Staffing of search rooms ranges from one to six. It is usual to have one archivist available and at least one archive assistant. Ten offices have a sole archivist on duty who also produces the documents, and in four offices another member of staff takes sole charge. In the 1989 report *Standards of archive provision in London boroughs* only 11 respondents (37%) said that their search rooms were permanently supervised. Conversely, in Dundee all staff work in the search room because there is no space for them to work elsewhere in the building.

Security

Security has been considerably tightened over the past decade. CARN tickets have also contributed to security in the offices in which they have been introduced.

Reprographics

Charges range from 5p to £2 (median 20p) for A4 photocopies or printouts, from 10p to 50p (median 20p) for a microfilm frame, from 18p to £5 (median £1.08) for a duplicate fiche and from no charge to £35 for handling charges. Some offices are clearly offering a subsidised service. Other offices do not have the machinery for producing printouts from microform. Eleven offices allow self-service photocopies, usually of selected items only.

Twenty-two offices supply microform copies (17 shire counties and Birmingham, Gwent, Hackney, London Guildhall and Tyne & Wear). At least four more offices offer reprographic services but were unable to supply figures. In 1991/92 thirteen offices supplied original microforms (mean average of 4,769 supplied), eight provided duplicate microfilms (mean average 10,280) and 10 supplied duplicate microfiche (1,990). Figures for the number of photocopies supplied were not provided by many services outside the shire and Welsh counties, so the resultant mean average of 11,550 is probably rather too high.

Table 6

Security measures

The figures given in brackets are the number of repositories planning to introduce measures:

| | English Counties | | English Districts/Boroughs | | | | | | |
	Shire	Metro	Shire	London	Metro	Wales	Scotland	Guernsey	Total
No of returns	38	9	7	12	17	5	10	1	99
Bags prohibited	32(2)	7	4	4	6	5	3	1	62(2)
Counting documents in/out	25	4	4	3	15	2	4	1	58
Closed circuit TV	10(3)	1	0	0(1)	3	1(1)	1	0	16(5)
Weighing machines	5(2)	3	0	0	2	0(1)	0	0	10(3)

Research services

All but nine repositories undertake research on behalf of correspondents but 41 make charges for in-depth research requiring information from documents. Charges range from £5 to £30 per hour but are usually between £12 and £15. Higher charges are imposed by some offices for research undertaken for legal and/or business clients. Eighteen offices (15 in the shire counties, two in London and one in Wales) now have self-financing genealogical researchers, a considerable increase since 1984, when only two were noted. Self-financing operations can be problematic when there are peaks and troughs in demand. In Essex, an advertisement in *Family Tree* magazine boosted business, and casual labour is called upon in peak times when waiting times become unacceptable. However, self-funded researchers offer a more comprehensive service than is usually possible when no charge is made for the service, and also free other staff to cope, for example, with the increasing numbers of visitors in the search room.

Customer orientation

Customer care initiatives have been introduced in many archive services. Forty-one offices have procedures for testing user satisfaction with their services and eight more are planning to introduce them. Complaints/comments/compliments forms are available in many of these repositories. Well-advertised complaints procedures and the holding of regular meetings of search room staff to analyse complaints and ideas for improvement were also reported. In Essex and Berkshire regular meetings are held with the local family history societies. The introduction of customer charters by 15 offices has led to a further re-examination of services offered to the public, such as the speed of responses to letters and reprographic orders. Charters are usually introduced as part of a council-wide policy.

User surveys have been undertaken in 37 repositories and are under consideration in five more. They follow a common formula of finding out about visitors and their expectations, and asking about satisfaction levels with various aspects of the service. Some offices use the opportunity to canvass opinion on future policy changes such as the extension or alteration of opening hours, the introduction of admission charges, facilities desired by searchers in a new record office, or priority areas for extra resources. Some user surveys have been sent to local historical and genealogical societies, which broadens the scope, particularly as they usually include some potential searchers who have not yet used record offices for a variety of reasons. Analysis of the surveys has led to changes in many offices, such as the introduction of name badges and more friendly rules, the re-examination of photocopy procedures, and the re-arrangement of accommodation to make room for more desks or a rest room for users. It has been discovered by several offices that a high percentage of visitors are first time users (e.g. 33% in Hampshire) and family history starter packs, beginners' afternoons, simplified guides, and the clearer labelling, colour coding and clarification of finding aids are being introduced as a result.

Many offices incorporate columns in their visitors' books or registration cards to allow regular analysis of user profiles. Fifty-seven repositories provided information about their user profiles and a mean average of 50% were family historians, 11% were in higher or further education, 8% were schoolchildren, and 9% were legal or business users. 36% came from outside the administrative area served by the record office. As confirmed by the 1990/91 statistics compiled by the Archivists of Scottish Local Authorities Working Group, Scottish user profiles are generally rather different with over 28% of visitors from the parent authorities and 23% family historians, 21% academics and 19% legal/business clients.

Changes requiring additional resources are being pursued by some offices, such as the extension of opening hours and the provision of limited services in the localities. In the past, some county record offices have opened branches to serve local communities or to continue an earlier service. A more recent alternative approach has been to supply microform or other copies of documents relating to a particular area for consultation in a local library or museum, or sometimes, as in Bedfordshire, in conjunction with a local society. Fifteen county record offices already provide microform copies to museums and libraries, and some, such as Cheshire and Hampshire, are considering building up this service. This approach has the advantage of satisfying 'local' researchers whilst maintaining, to maximum efficiency, the full range of source materials under one roof, a facility much appreciated by 'regional' researchers.

Performance indicators

This is probably the area where most progress has been made in the collection of data, the necessary prerequisite for performance indicators. The numbers of visitors, written and telephone enquiries, and documents produced are now recorded by most repositories, although the figures are not always as directly comparable between repositories as might at first appear. Reader figures occasionally include those attending talks, and school groups, particularly if such visitors are asked to sign the visitors' book from which the reader statistics are compiled. Some offices do not record statistics for self-service microform or cannot separate records management or microform productions from the number of archival items produced. In a few library-based services it is not currently possible to separate statistics for archival use from those for local studies or the rest of the library.

A number of performance indicators are in use, including the number of visitors per member of staff (full-time equivalent) servicing the public area; trends in visitor numbers compared with other offices, last month or last year; the number of productions per reader, member of staff or cubic metre of cataloged holdings; the number of times documents take longer to deliver than the advertised time, or have to be collected from an out-store; and the number of microform users as a percentage of the visitor total, for use in predicting future equipment needs.

User surveys enable offices to analyse user satisfaction, but cannot be used too often and thus only provide a picture of satisfaction at a particular point in time. Listening to users, analysing written and verbal complaints, and perhaps holding more formal consultation exercises provide additional means of measuring satisfaction levels.

9 Education

Curriculum changes

Archives have been used in the teaching of history for many years and some offices have a long-established tradition of helping children and teachers to interpret archives. At Essex, the first education officer was appointed in 1946, for example. However, a much greater challenge now faces record offices following the replacement in England and Wales from 1986 to 1988 of the GCE 'O' level by the GCSE with its emphasis on experiential learning through the use of original sources. This was followed closely by the introduction, under the 1988 Education Reform Act, of the National Curriculum, which also promoted the use of documentary sources for history and geography. The increasing emphasis on resource-based syllabuses and investigative approaches can also be seen in Scotland in the new Standard Grade which replaced 'O' Grade. Changes to Scottish primary syllabuses with the integration of history into environmental studies have also generated demand for 'local studies' material.

Archive education services

The response of record offices to this new challenge has been remarkably varied across the country. Of the 96 respondents, only 39 claimed to run an education service, but it was clear from the comments that many more archivists were responding as best they could to educational demand, even if no formal service was offered. For instance, Southampton has received visits of 'school teachers (with or without children) to look at documents and prepare material for use in class' and has booked separate rooms in the civic centre when numbers have been too great to fit into the search room. A few offices have joined with museums and/or education departments to provide, though not necessarily fund, a joint education officer (e.g. Cheshire, Gwynedd, Warwickshire), and in Oxfordshire one of the leisure and arts department's education officers is attached to the Centre for Oxfordshire Studies and takes archives into his brief. A total of 20 responding record offices have their own education officer or share the services of one, which suggests that in the other 19 offices with an education service archivists are providing this on top of their other duties.

Nature of service

The nature of the education service provided varies considerably, from the largely reactive responses in offices without a formal service, where archivists have to cope with individual schoolchildren arriving in the search room without prior notice, and making unstructured, unrealistic requests, to the well-organised, pro-active services offered by education officers. Teachers across the country cannot, therefore, rely upon record offices to provide a standard set of services.

The number of talks or teaching sessions given by education officers ranged from 5 to 824 (mean 76, median 30). Total attendance during the year ranged from 192 to 41,274 (this was achieved in Essex), with mean 5,496 and median 1,555. Wide variations in the target groups and thus in the use of the record office by different educational users were apparent. Primary schools comprised from 5% to 90%, secondary schools from 3% to 70% and higher and further education from 0% to 80% of record offices' educational users. The median averages were 50% primary schools, 25% secondary schools and 25% higher or further education. The predominance of primary schools is perhaps explained by the more extensive use of local resources in teaching at key stages 1 and 2 as most subjects start from the child's own area and personal experience. There are also many more primary schools and fewer history specialists teaching in them. In some offices, such as Essex, Strathclyde and Warwickshire, sixth formers and students are generally dealt with by archivists as it is felt that historical interpretation and advice on sources are more important than teaching skills.

The predominance, or otherwise, of teaching in record offices' education programmes depends to some extent on the nature of the teaching space available. Forty-three offices have rooms which can be used for educational purposes and a further four have access to suitable rooms. The seating capacity varies from 12 to 250 (median 30). Thirty seats is a good size for a class, but many offices have rooms too small to accommodate a whole class. In Cumbria, map rooms are used in Carlisle and Kendal, and Barrow manages by using a sorting room as necessary. Some offices (e.g. Bolton, Tameside) receive school groups on days when the search room is closed to the public, or concentrate instead on taking the service out to the schools (e.g. Bedfordshire, Durham). In contrast, in Tyne & Wear more groups are being encouraged to visit the record office, where facilities are good.

Some services which seek to meet the needs of several hundred schools have concluded that the teaching of individual pupils, or indeed groups of pupils, is no longer an appropriate response. The problem is particularly acute in Strathclyde which includes approximately half the school-age population in Scotland. Resources are instead channelled into the production of archive resource packs. In England and Wales, the National Curriculum has made it possible to anticipate demand to a much greater extent and old resources have been reclassified to tie in directly with the new syllabuses in a number of offices. Complementary computer disks have also been produced by some of the more advanced services. In Scotland, demand is less easy to predict, but areas of likely demand have been projected in Strathclyde by the education officer in conjunction with the region's history advisers. The need to help teachers interpret resources produced was reiterated by a number of offices visited.

The training of teachers in the use of archives is seen to be very important and most archive education officers make regular contributions to in-service training programmes. Sessions for trainee teachers are also organised. In some offices emphasis is placed on the training of teachers rather than children. It is felt to be more effective to work with a group of 15 teachers, for example, than a class of 15 pupils, particularly when there is only one officer to cover 800 schools, as in Hampshire.

Another method of spreading the resources more widely is employed in Warwickshire where the education officer and an archivist have trained four project leaders who now compile resource packs, make presentations to school classes and offer a search service for teachers who are unable to visit the record office but want specially tailored packs of local resources.

The importance of liaison with others who are providing similar services was emphasised in follow-up visits. A number of co-operative ventures have been undertaken: for example, history advisers in Gwynedd disseminated to schools computer disks produced by the education officers. Cross-curricular approaches also seem to be appreciated, particularly by primary schools.

Although there are differences in emphasis, the archive education officers visited are providing a broad cross-section of the following elements: teaching/training; resource production/publication; interpretation/display; and liaison. In the light of the introduction of resource-based syllabuses and Local Management of Schools (see below), it is vital for archive education services to provide what the teachers require. The dangers of failing to do so are that funding could be diverted elsewhere, that archives could be marginalised, or that schools could start collecting archives or wearing out their own log books and other records through over-use. If schools are to be persuaded to deposit their documents, it is important for record offices to respond flexibly to the demands of the teachers.

Thirty offices ran adult education classes during 1991/92 and several more reported that staff ran classes at venues other than the record office or that they had run classes in the recent past or were planning to do so in the future. The evening classes were often run as private enterprises in the archivists' spare time, but they obviously filled a gap in demand from adults for education in local or family history, palaeography or interpretation of primary source material, and also served an important outreach function for the record office.

Funding

Five of the education officers were jointly funded, usually by the record office and the education or museums department, but in Bedfordshire a local charity provided one third of the funding. Eight were funded entirely by their education department and seven by the record office. Funding by education departments enabled Essex and Strathclyde to provide resources free to schools. Education departments also provided close links with inspectors and sometimes secretarial and computer support.

The gradual introduction in England and Wales of Local Management of Schools (LMS), shifting resources away from central education departments to individual schools and colleges, and the increasing number of schools opting out of local authority control, is beginning to have an effect on some services. Cutbacks in local education budgets have led to the withdrawal of funding for archive education officers in Coventry and Lincolnshire and will take effect in Bedfordshire from April 1993. Charges have already been introduced by some archive education services, although these are by no means uniform. Resource packs can be distributed free or cost as much as £90 and all schools in Warwickshire are charged for National Curriculum teaching units. In Somerset, schools have already been reallocated budgets for purchasing centrally provided education services, and 67% have opted to buy archive services. Those schools not subscribing to the scheme are charged for all services; a charge of £3.50 is levied per 15 minutes consultation per schoolchild, for instance. Private schools are charged in some counties, are given a free service in others, and are not provided with a service at all in at least one region. Similarly universities and teacher training and other colleges are given a free service by most education officers, but are not provided for in at least one county because no funding is forthcoming.

Other sources of funding

The National Curriculum has stimulated a demand for new resources and teachers are at the same time encouraged to look for quality products. Quality is sometimes equated with the quality of the paper or printing or the price being asked. Several officers remarked on a tendency for teachers to buy national publications rather than local resources of poorer quality reproduction. West Sussex is responding to the demand by producing glossy resources, but other offices have found funding difficult. In Gwynedd a joint bid to the Welsh Office for £8,000 to produce a National Curriculum resource pack (of printed documents, teachers' notes and a computer disk) has been successful. In Essex, the Friends of Historic Essex paid for the development of model local studies packs.

Performance indicators

Performance indicators can help in assessing whether the right service is being offered. Monitoring the use of individual school packs and teaching units, for example, gives a good idea of which ones are best meeting the teachers' needs. It is difficult to calculate how many children a particular archive education officer has reached as teachers helped probably take back their knowledge to the whole history department as well as their own class. However, the recording of the number of talks, courses or teaching sessions given, the number of children at National Curriculum, GCSE, 'A' level and HE/FE levels, and the number of records used provide a useful basis. Additional measures could include the number of resources produced, use of the search room by individual schoolchildren following up group visits, and possibly time spent on the various activities.

10 Outreach

Only seven respondents submitted written outreach policies but articles in the *Journal of the Society of Archivists* by Chris Weir from Nottinghamshire, Nigel Yates from Kent and Gareth Haulfryn Williams from Gwynedd (12 (1991), 15-25; 9 (1988), 69-75; and 10 (1989), 57-65, 155-61 respectively) all indicate well thoughtout policies. Several services, including West Yorkshire and Essex, have designated 'promotions officers' or archivists specifically responsible for outreach. A number of services reported that outreach work was in abeyance due to staffing problems or other pressures, such as moving premises.

Talks

Archivists have traditionally regarded their programme of talks as the cornerstone of their outreach policy. Indeed only eight offices offered no talks in the period 1991/92 and these were all small offices with few staff. The average number of talks given per office was 15 (median) to 23 (mean) with an average attendance ranging from seven to 62.5. Many offices, particularly those covering smaller areas such as Portsmouth and Anglesey, regard talks as vital for spreading the word about the office, encouraging accessions, creating goodwill, and recruiting volunteers. In offices which cover a huge geographical area such as Strathclyde, the effectiveness of talks, which can only reach a minute fraction of their catchment area, is being questioned and more emphasis is being placed on using the media. Other offices reported that talks were limited in some way, such as one per week, or one per year for a particular society, general talks on the work of the office only, specifically targeted groups such as local or family historians or clergymen, or groups not touched before. A survey carried out by the Tyne & Wear Archives Service showed that only 1% of their users had found out about the record office through the talks programme, and Gareth Haulfryn Williams concluded (*Journal of the Society of Archivists*, 10 (1989), 58-9) that spending evenings speaking to small social groups was unacceptably time-consuming and not cost-effective.

Media

Sixty-four repositories reported that they regularly used newspapers, 54 local radio, 33 television, in their outreach programmes. The recent proliferation of local free sheets and local radio stations has made coverage easier. Several offices (e.g. Gwynedd, Northumberland and Oxfordshire) noted that a member of staff had regular spots on radio or television. Where offices are situated on television or radio station borders or where there is no truly local service, as in parts of London, record office initiatives are less successful.

Exhibitions

Exhibitions, like talks, are another traditional method used by archivists to promote greater awareness of record offices, their collections and services. All but 14 staged exhibitions in 1991/92 and the 92 responding record offices provided a total of 609 exhibitions between them. A purely numerical comparison of the number of exhibitions produced by different record offices is not helpful as the scale of exhibitions varies considerably.

In order to create a good impression and compare favourably with the high quality exhibitions produced by other bodies, some record offices have employed designers and used a full range of marketing techniques or have organised joint exhibitions, particularly where they attract grants or sponsorship. Some give priority to exhibitions which can be toured in the locality or even abroad. Gwynedd's archival exhibitions have been toured by the Area Museum Council and Essex charges £100 for the hire of exhibitions to cover travelling costs. An exhibitions catalogue is circulated to potential venues, giving an idea of the exhibitions available and including specifications for those wishing to hire an exhibition to fill a gap in their own exhibitions programme. Exhibitions produced in Essex often link in with the county council's projects and form an important part of the corporate policy of promotions and public relations.

At the other end of the spectrum, many offices concentrate on small-scale, but time-consuming, exhibitions such as facsimile boards of parish or school records which have been requested for anniversaries. At least one office has taken a policy decision not to undertake exhibitions as they cannot be produced to the high standards expected by the public.

Publications

Fifty-three offices produce publications, ranging from family history leaflets, and guides to classes of records, to high quality academic publications. Facsimile maps and posters and books of old photographs also feature regularly. Fourteen repositories produce both annual reports and newsletters, 23 annual reports only and eight newsletters only.

Some of the publications have specific target groups, such as folders on black and women's history produced in Lambeth as part of the Equal Opportunities Policy, or the books on ethnic communities produced in Hammersmith & Fulham in conjunction with an active oral history group in an attempt to find out more about communities for whom the documentary evidence is slight. The market for the six-monthly newsletter produced by Essex has been carefully researched. Three thousand copies were printed, of which 2,000 were paid for by the Family History Society, 450 were distributed to the Friends of Historic Essex, 200 were paid for by subscribers and the rest were on sale in the record office bookshop or distributed to committee members and local history societies. Market research and advance orders by subscription have also dictated the price and number of local history videos produced by Chester as part of an income generation programme.

Income generation from publications appears to be frequently regarded as secondary to the outreach role or the provision of a service to users and to local history in general. Some criticised the clogging up of strongrooms or other storage areas with over-ambitious print runs. Effective marketing was seen to be vital and both Essex and Gwynedd have shop cum exhibition areas, good quality publication catalogues, press release programmes and members of staff or students who take stock to bookshops in the county. Museums and libraries provide additional outlets.

Friends

Twenty-three repositories reported having Friends organisations. The majority (15) are concentrated in the shire counties, and a further three are planned. At least six Friends organisations (Cumbria, Dorset, Oxfordshire, Shropshire, East Sussex and Warwickshire) have been established in the counties since Rosemary Dunhill's survey in 1988 (*Journal of the Society of Archivists*, 10 (1989), 75-80). Some of the districts have thriving groups. The talks run by the Dundee Friends have attracted attendances of over 100, for example, and the long established Portsmouth Friends group provides the record office with about 40 volunteers. Membership levels range from 99 to 398 individual members or households. The Hampshire Archives Trust is the only body to have a substantial number (83) of corporate members. Some Friends organisations are largely independent of the record office but others are run by the office to which they are attached. Lectures, visits, newsletters and social events are often organised by or for the Friends. In return, the Friends provide valuable support or lobby groups, volunteer labour, financial contributions and useful channels of communication and publicity.

Other outreach activities

The following activities form an important part of the outreach policies of some offices: local history fairs (e.g. Portsmouth, Tyne & Wear, West Yorkshire); archive road shows, taken to locations where the record offices do not have a strong presence (e.g. Berkshire, Essex, Gloucestershire, Nottinghamshire); open days or weeks (e.g. Hampshire, Lambeth, Greater Manchester, Tyne & Wear); family history surgeries (e.g. Chester); oral history groups or training days (e.g. Hammersmith & Fulham, Hampshire) and children's activities, where the parents are the main target (e.g. Chester, Portsmouth).

The question about surveys for other record-holding bodies was answered inconsistently so has not been analysed.

Performance indicators

Since a great deal of staff time and financial resources can be dedicated to an outreach policy, particularly if active exhibition and publication programmes are undertaken, the production of a written statement of aims and objectives, together with the adoption of performance measures would seem vital. The Society of Archivists' Working Party on Performance Indicators and Standards recommends that 'the statement might usefully make clear which of [the outreach] activities are directed towards improving services to the employing authority, which to attracting new acquisitions, assisting existing readers/searches and definable interest groups, and which to attracting new readers'. At Chester, outreach activities are analysed both before they are undertaken and after the event, by asking a series of questions such as: 'Why are we doing this activity? Are we providing what is required? Are we trying to generate income as well as gain publicity? Are we promoting a good or bad image of the record office? Was it worth it? How do we know whether we were successful?' A bookmark with a section to be returned (for an entry into a free draw) gives a further indication of where outreach activities have been successful. User questionnaires, or asking new users how they have found out about the record office are other ways of measuring the success of outreach activities.

11 Finance

Nature of replies

In 1992, as in 1984, the financial section of the questionnaire produced the least reliable responses. Part of the reason lies in the fact that 31 out of 92 head archivists do not control their own budgets. Thirteen services were unable to supply salary statistics, 27 buildings expenditure and 20 other expenditure, whilst 20 offices could not provide figures for income. One Scottish repository was asked by its authority not to supply figures as they were deemed confidential. West Glamorgan was only established as a separate record service in April 1992 so no figures are available.

Separating costs directly attributable to the archive service has proved difficult for a number of services, particularly those based in libraries. Typical is Stockport's reply that archival building costs and photocopy income cannot be separated from the library's budget, and that library staff answer letters and retrieve documents. There are also many hidden subsidies in overheads subsumed in larger headings, as indicated clearly when head archivists entered nil for expenditure on buildings or other expenses. Similarly, publications programmes and computerisation costs are sometimes borne on a wider vote and not recorded in archival budgets. The number of footnotes and provisos in the returns also indicates a wide range of accounting procedures amongst employing bodies which do not make cost comparisons between archive services very reliable.

Expenditure

Although the capital expenditure on new archive buildings was not covered by the questionnaire, local authorities, mainly in England and Wales, have invested large sums in state-of-the-art, purpose-built record offices and conversions and extensions over the past decade. Over 50 local authority record offices have been built, extended or adapted in the period 1980-1990. The initial capital cost of building and equipping a medium-sized repository can now be expected to amount to between £2 and £3 million (*Twenty-seventh report of the Royal Commission on Historical Manuscripts 1982-1990*, 1992, p.32).

Expenditure on the maintenance of buildings varied from nil (where the costs of heating, lighting etc. are obviously borne centrally) to £357,237. Taking into consideration only those respondents who supplied full figures for expenditure, the mean average expenditure on buildings maintenance was £79,650, 23% of the archival budget. This is likely to be an underestimate of average expenditure as so many services based in libraries or in shared administrative premises are clearly subsidised or not recharged at all for central accommodation. Expenditure in the London boroughs was very much lower than the national average.

The salary returns are not entirely reliable because some offices counted on-costs, but the Society of Archivists salary statistics 1991/92 have been used to remove obvious discrepancies. The main conclusion to be drawn is that salaries form a very high proportion of all archive services' budgets. Excluding revenue expenditure on buildings (which was largely beyond the head archivists' control) salaries comprised a mean average of £163,274, 69% of an archive service's budget, and would have been slightly higher if on-costs had been included. In the less well developed services in Scotland, salaries comprised 79% of expenditure. Such high percentages have particularly severe implications when local authorities introduce cuts across the board. Redundancies, the freezing of vacant posts or the reduction of hours of part-time staff are often the only solutions where there is so little room for manoeuvre in the rest of the budget. Such measures have been employed in Hammersmith & Fulham, Lambeth and Warwickshire, for example.

Expenditure on conservation ranged from nil to £24,515 (median £2,450, mean £4,065). Conservation averaged between 5% (median) and 14% (mean) of expenditure not devoted to buildings and salaries. The proportion was much higher in Perth & Kinross (92%) but lower in the metropolitan districts where five repositories spent nothing on conservation. Document purchase, assisted by grant aid, fluctuates from year to year. In 1991/92, expenditure ranged from nil to £100,997 (median £1,000, mean £6,846 if only those repositories which purchased documents are taken into account). Document purchase averaged between 2% (median) and 8% (mean) of these repositories' expenditure excluding buildings and salaries. An analysis of expenditure on computer development is difficult because many record offices rely wholly or in part on their employing body's information technology department and are often not recharged for such services. A total of 44 offices have information technology (IT) votes and a further 16 offices were unable to provide a figure for their expenditure on IT. Expenditure ranged from nil to £47,082 (the latter sum includes investment in capital equipment and software development and as such is a one-off expense). Considering only those repositories which spent money on IT in 1991/92, the median expenditure was £2,945 and the mean £7,031 and IT comprised between 5% (median) and 14% (mean) of expenditure excluding buildings and salaries.

Income

Income varied from nil to £129,550. Twenty respondents could not supply a figure. The median figure was £11,368 and the median percentage that income comprised of total archival budgets (including salaries and buildings) was 5%. Higher income figures were nearly all accounted for by the receipt of grant aid for document purchase or conservation, contributions received for the maintenance of shared services (e.g. Morpeth Records Centre in Northumberland and conservation for the library service in Lancashire), or the recharging of departments for records management services. No separate figures were requested for recharges. Grant aid amounted to £97,692 in Cornwall (85% of the income of that office). Thirty-one offices reported that they had benefited from some form of grant aid in 1991/92 (median £2,494, mean £12,549). This comprised 19% (median) to 33% (mean) of total income of these offices.

Many services reported that they had come under pressure from their employing bodies to undertake more income generating activities, or were moving in that direction themselves. Three services - Devon, Gloucestershire and Lincolnshire - had introduced charges which raised as much as £8,190 in Devon in 1991/92. This represented 32% of the income generated by that office but only 2% of the total archive expenditure. Greater Manchester had introduced entry charges for Stockport residents as a result of this district's withdrawal of financial backing for the county-wide archive service. Other record offices rigorously upheld the principle of free access and concentrated instead on other methods of income generation. Donations were encouraged in most offices and ranged from £10 to £8,000, but they only produced an average of between 3% (median) and 11% (mean) of the total income generated.

Publications are often regarded as income generating and large sums were occasionally recorded in this section of the questionnaire, eg. £26,478 at Essex. However, these usually represented turnover rather than profit so no further analysis was carried out except to note that 49 offices had publications budgets and a further 23 were unable to provide either profit or turnover figures arising from their publications programme. The provision of copies of documents was undertaken by all but three services and an average of £2,170 (median) or £5,620 (mean) of archival income was raised in this way, and comprised between 31% (median) and 40% (mean) of income. In West Yorkshire £53,456 was received from this source, and in Rotherham, 92% of the service's income was derived from copies. In order to work out the true value of copying to an income generating programme it would be necessary to deduct costs expended in providing this service. In services which levied research fees, the sums raised varied from £20 to £61,301 (median £2,807, mean £5,959) and comprised between 14% (median) and 21% (mean) of income.

Business planning

Thirty-eight offices have produced business or medium term plans. The scale of the plans varies from the identification of key targets to an in-depth analysis of all the functions and resources of the record office. The plans generally deal with resource allocation, policy planning and the setting and monitoring of realistic goals. They are often, but not always, closely linked to the repository's budget bid.

Conclusion

The survey has indicated that local government archive services are on the whole better resourced than they were a decade ago, but that improvements have not taken place evenly across the country. Some services, particularly a number of the smaller ones, are severely under-resourced. Despite an increasing emphasis on income generation, there is no prospect of a local authority archive service becoming self-financing. Conclusions and comparisons are difficult because of differing financial conventions in different authorities. In some cases these prevent the archivists themselves from having a full knowledge of the costs of their service. Such a knowledge will become increasingly important in the climate of competitive tendering, compulsory or otherwise, and possible local government reorganisation. Section 1.6 of the Historical Manuscripts Commission's *A standard for record repositories* states: 'The archivist in charge should be responsible to the governing body for an identifiable annual budget'. The adoption of this recommendation by all archive services may well become more realistic as many councils move towards devolved financial management.

12   Quality, standards and performance indicators

During the 1980s there has been a growth of interest, promoted by the Audit Commission, in the concept of performance in local government. The growing number of local government services being subjected to compulsory competitive tendering, the quest for quality following the promotion in 1990 of section 8 of BS 5750 *Guide to quality management and quality systems elements for services,* and the Citizen's Charter initiative of 1991, have provided further incentives to move in this direction. Forty-seven record offices are planning, or have already introduced, a quality system and/or some performance indicators.

Standards and quality

Standards form the basis of all quality systems. Archivists are fortunate in having two national standards: BS 5454 *Recommendations for storage and exhibition of archival documents* (1977, revised 1989) and the Historical Manuscripts Commission's *A standard for record repositories on constitution and finance, staff, acquisition, access* (1990). Fifty-one local authority archive services reported that they had subscribed to the 1990 *Standard.* Other 'good practice' standards are laid down in the draft *Guideline* of the Society of Archivists' Working Party on Performance Indicators and Standards. Questionnaire responses show that several of these standards have already been adopted by many services. For example, 51% have policy statements, 61% written acquisitions policies, 91% accessions registers, and 59% receipt forms.

In Berkshire 'measurable and achievable' standards are being drafted for areas such as cataloguing, conservation, storage and customer care, partly in preparation for a departmental quality audit. The Wirral archivist has drawn up a quality assurance manual which lays down standards and procedures covering the major areas of record office activities. None of the archivists asked are planning to seek accreditation under BS 5750 but some intend to make use of it when assessing the quality of their services and products.

Performance indicators

An examination of the performance indicators used in the offices visited has revealed substantial benefits: help in assigning priorities, planning services and managing resources; better methods of assessing whether customer demands are being met (e.g. in education and user services), or otherwise measuring the effectiveness of services (e.g. outreach) and of professional activity levels (e.g. cataloguing); and better methods of costing policy implementation (e.g. in records management and conservation). Performance indicators also enable managers to compare performance with pre-set targets or with other archive services, and to analyse trends over time. However, the statistics and information systems require improvement and standardisation in many areas before accurate comparisons between archive services will be possible.

The revised performance indicators recommended by the Society's Working Party are not intended to be prescriptive, but instead comprise a menu from which an appropriate selection can be made by any repository, from the manuscripts department of a university library to a business archive. Even within the local government context to which the present survey has been restricted, marked variations in practice occur. The standardisation of some practices, especially relating to income and expenditure, lies outside the control of the professional archivists concerned. But the greater the number of offices adopting a substantial package of the same measures, the easier it will be in the future to make helpful comparisons.

13 Conclusion

Since the last survey in 1985, local authorities as a whole have demonstrated a substantial commitment to preserving the archival heritage by providing increased resources and a large number of new buildings. Record offices themselves have worked hard to attract additional funds from elsewhere, mainly for cataloguing and conservation, whilst also ensuring that their existing resources can be used to best effect by undertaking business planning and surveys of cataloguing and conservation backlogs. Performance indicators will have an increasingly important role to play in this area as they come to be adopted more widely. Record offices now have more readers, more enquiries and more archives than eight years ago and many have taken on new functions and offer a wider range of higher quality services in spheres such as customer care, self-financing research, computerised lists and indexes, and improved packaging for archives.

However, another very clear conclusion is that the level of archive provision is uneven across the country. Certain repositories are centres of excellence in the fields of records management, education, outreach and film and sound provision, for example. Others, particularly some of the smaller repositories in London, the metropolitan districts and Scotland, have insufficient staff or finances to meet increasing demands on them. Lack of conservators, lack of environmental controls in strongrooms, and too few staff to tackle cataloguing backlogs, to survey and rescue records, or to provide an appropriate response to demands from educational users, remain problems in several offices. The Historical Manuscripts Commission's *A standard for record repositories* provides a useful benchmark to which many have subscribed, and it is hoped that others will follow in order to improve the general level of archive provision.

The new district and borough archive services set up in metropolitan areas since the last survey are still in an early stage of development, but many remain understaffed. Some of the former metropolitan counties have maintained strong and efficient services, but in others earlier progress has been compromised. The need to maintain voluntary co-operative services has imposed its strain and made forward planning more difficult, especially in the sphere of capital expenditure.

These lessons are very relevant in the context of the current review of local government. The survey shows healthy growth resulting from commitment from staff, elected members and the general public. It is vital that the unique position and importance of local authority archive services should be protected and allowed to develop, regardless of successive changes in the structure of local government.

Appendix

Record repositories to which the questionnaire was sent

Names in brackets indicate those from which no return was received. Those in bold type indicate offices to which follow-up visits were made.

ENGLAND

Shire counties

Bedfordshire
Berkshire
Buckinghamshire
Cambridgeshire
  Cambridge
  Huntingdon
Cheshire
Cleveland
Cornwall
Cumbria
  Carlisle
  Barrow
  Kendal
Derbyshire
Devon
  Exeter
  Barnstaple
  Plymouth
Dorset
(Durham)
Essex
  Chelmsford
  Colchester
  Southend
Gloucestershire
Hampshire
Hereford & Worcester
  Worcester
  Hereford
Hertfordshire
(Humberside)
  (Beverley)
  (Grimsby)
(Kent)
  (Maidstone)
  (Canterbury)
  (Folkestone)
  (Ramsgate)
  Rochester
  (Sevenoaks)
Lancashire
Leicestershire
Lincolnshire
Norfolk
Northamptonshire

Northumberland
  Newcastle
  Berwick upon Tweed
Nottinghamshire
Oxfordshire
Shropshire
Somerset
Staffordshire
  Stafford
  Lichfield
Suffolk
  Ipswich
  Bury St Edmunds
  Lowestoft
Surrey
  Kingston upon Thames
  Guildford
East Sussex
West Sussex
Warwickshire
Isle of Wight
Wiltshire
North Yorkshire

Metropolitan counties

(Greater London)
Greater Manchester
Merseyside
Tyne & Wear
West Yorkshire
  Wakefield
  Bradford
  Calderdale
  Kirklees
  Leeds
  Yorkshire Archaeological
    Society

Shire districts

Bath
Bristol
Chester
Hull
Portsmouth
Southampton
(Warrington Library)
York

London boroughs etc

Corporation of London

33

Guildhall Library
(Barnet)
(Bexley)
(Brent)
(Bromley)
(Camden)
  (Swiss Cottage)
  (Holborn)
Croydon
Greenwich
Hackney
Hammersmith & Fulham
Haringey
(Kensington & Chelsea)
Lambeth
Lewisham
Newham
(Redbridge)
(Southwark)
Sutton
(Tower Hamlets)
(Waltham Forest)
Westminster
  Victoria Library
  Marylebone Library

Metropolitan districts

Barnsley
Birmingham
Bolton
Bury
(Coventry)
Doncaster
Dudley
Knowsley
Liverpool
(Manchester)
Oldham
(Rochdale)
Rotherham
(St Helens)
(Salford)
(Sandwell)
(Sefton)
Stockport
Sheffield
Tameside
Walsall
Wigan
Wirral
Wolverhampton

WALES

Counties

Clwyd
  Hawarden
  Ruthin
(Dyfed)
  (Carmarthen)
  (Aberystwyth)
  (Haverfordwest)
(Glamorgan)
West Glamorgan
Gwent
Gwynedd
  Caernarfon
  Dolgellau
  Llangefni
Powys

(City)
(Swansea)

SCOTLAND

Regions and islands

Borders
(Central)
(Dumfries & Galloway)
Grampian
Highland
Orkney
(Shetland)
Strathclyde

Districts

(Aberdeen)
(Angus)
(Argyll & Bute)
Dundee
Edinburgh
Glasgow, Mitchell Library
(Moray)
Nithsdale
Perth and Kinross

(ISLE OF MAN)

GUERNSEY

Printed in the United Kingdom for HMSO

Dd 293669 1/93 C10 3396 17434